Chrysanthemum, Chrysanthemum

Nadine Sabra Meyer

New Issues Poetry & Prose

A Green Rose Book

New Issues Poetry & Prose
The College of Arts and Sciences
Western Michigan University
Kalamazoo, Michigan 49008

Printed in the United States of America.

First Edition, 2017.

ISBN: 978-1-936970-46-9 (paperbound)

Library of Congress Cataloging-in-Publication Data:
Sabra Meyer, Nadine.
Chrysanthemum, Chrysanthemum/Nadine Sabra Meyer
Library of Congress Control Number: 2016919570

Editor:	William Olsen
Managing Editor:	Kimberly Kolbe
Layout Editor:	Sarah Kidd
Assistant Editor:	Ephraim Sommers
Art Direction:	Nicholas Kuder
Design:	Carla Sofia Zorrilla Baquero
Image:	Mussel Memories and a Coral Fixation © Duy Huynh
Production:	Paul Sizer The Design Center, Frostic School of Art College of Fine Arts Western Michigan University
Printing:	McNaughton & Gunn, Inc.

Chrysanthemum, Chrysanthemum

Nadine Sabra Meyer

New Issues
WESTERN MICHIGAN UNIVERSITY

Also by Nadine Sabra Meyer

The Anatomy Theater (HarperCollins, winner of the National Poetry Series)

For Chloe

& in memory of my parents, Marilyn Pettit (1931-2009)
and Jean-Pierre Meyer (1929-2013)

Contents

I

Shelley on His Funeral Pyre	5
And then	7
The Dolls' House	9
Atrium	10
Invocation: A Fragment	11
The Shower	12
The Shutting	14
Apple of the Earth: A Fairytale	16
Go	17
Sanctuary: A Premonition	18
The umbrella mass	19
Shadow Boxes	20
Prayer	22
Night Aria on the Widow's Walk	24
A Toast	26
Morning after a Stormy Night	27

II

Requiem	31
Elegy with Fossilized Sharks' Teeth	32
Unraveling Her Web	34
Adoration	35
A Woman Weighing Gold	36
Woman and Child Blowing Bubbles	37
The Lace-Maker's Bloom	38
In the Garage	39
The Legible Body: or Melancholia	41
Prayer 2	43
Cartography	45
The Portrait Miniature	47
The Body: or Breach	49
The Beekeeper's Daughter	51
The Telephone Call	53
Horse and Rider	55
Effacement	56
Interior with Calder Mobile	57

One.

Shelley on His Funeral Pyre

As breakers storm the shore and the cords beneath him sound his fall—
that catastrophic movement, full-bodied, orchestral,
we all come to in the end, the embrace of body to burn, to consumption,
the self-extinguishment of cell and calorie—beneath him
bark peeling like finger tips, Shelley lies afloat
in his hair, his face soot stained like a man at work
in his dying, death like a hardening
of the mind's arteries. Today all day doctors mined
my father's arteries, took him in hand, and, the way
you break a crab down its stem-line, halved him.
The shell of his breastbone open, they snaked
stents through his body's ducts, until they reached
the grotto, four chambered, thundering,
and there pierced, like toothpicks to the avocado's seed,
four stents to the heart's core. Hospital bed or pyre,
love's the only bulwark against dying. My father
would lift me to the window's sill, where an avocado's seed, suspended
on the rim of the glass, would, with luck, grow.
Childhood is full of such suspensions. Each morning I lift
my daughter from our bed, and, her face bright with knowledge,
she shows me the first word she learned, the sign
we have—she opens and closes her fist as I carry her
to the kitchen—this word she knows I know she knows,
her fingers opening, spreading: *light*, *light*, *light*. In the painting
Shelley is burning; all is darkness, but the smoke
drawn through him, through his ashen face, and by that hoary light
you can see him suctioned from himself like oxygen
from the vial in Boyle's experiment with the air-pump,
the shaft suddenly a vacuum and, to prove it,
though you see no change in the glass, the cockatoo swivels, writhes:
suddenly brittle, a dusty ball. Five months now, each day all day,
a rope around my neck and shoulder secures me to you,
drowning man I try to drag to the surface
where our daughter plays. I used to hold you in the night,
my hand in the dent of your breastbone, our small bed,
the threadbare sheets, a raft. You said once,
we marry so someone will be there when we die. When Shelley died
his lungs were calibrated with flood water, his windpipe
whistled its narrow bamboo tone. Alone I drive home from the hospital;

your mind's caught you in a great sodden net, nettled
you in bottom-muck and seaweed. It was thought, once, the soul
inhabited the base of the mind, and, weighing the body before
and after the last tidal roar deep in the spiral
shell's oracle, all instruments meticulously tuned as surf scattered
to blood-pool and vapor atomized off the dying—philosophers
came to know the soul's weight, weight of the sliver of a finger nail.
Love's a bird's egg nested three-quarters high in the body. In the hollow
of my chest, where the soul flickers, in the lantern
of my ribcage, I know already the skinned body of loss: the small chalice
of trust desecrated, wind whipping our narrow wood framed house.
When Shelley's pyre burned down past rib-splinter, organ-ash,
the stone of his heart wouldn't burn, and they gave that small pit
to his wife. A clover, my father's heart stutters through, clenches
its four petaled life. Someday, Love, the horizon will draw its machete
and, with ice-cinders and lime-ash, lance us from ourselves.
The only bulwark is death in dark waters, a sliver of moon printing the lake.

And then

the difficult listening, the mind
tuned to draw the thread
of blood stitched
to squire the find,
a quail squalling in a field of corn—
a barren, harvested sky,
the smell of lit fire. Ash,
and, on the wing, a sparrow, the lit, then unlit
rise and falling of its gait. *Ash*
to ash, my father says;
we should pour them on his father's
headstone, in an old French cemetery
where grave teeth break through
moldering earth. My daughter and I
turn the soil
of our garden, loosening
worms she collects in a jar, the stem crust
and slap, break of root-hairs
to press something new into the yard's
moist mouth. *Let's visit the garden*
we planted Grandma in, she says, and we do,
the hill my father, with his fluid-filled heart,
tried to climb,
my own pulse pounding
my forehead, as, in grief
and guilt, I kept seeing
the scene gone awry: in procession
to my mother's grave, my father,
his stumbling gait, his
one heart
congested to failure, the fall
and crumple by the grave
I chose high on the hill
so she could see far, the geese schooling
the pond, the bobbins
they make of water rings,
the greening humps and,
vaster, the bowl of blue

sky, crazed
in bleats and calls.
We beckoned a gardener, who jostled
my father up the cemetery slope
in something like a golf cart. Thank God
for the mercy of absurdity,
my father and I
looking at our shoes by my mother's grave.
I teach my daughter
to plant, to turn the mineral-rich
soil, but as we kneel in the backyard,
her skirt skimming
her smudged ankles, I see the glint
of an old colander, and upturning it
uncorks the earth before us, dry soil
sifting down like sand
through a sieve, and a hole,
a shaft, large enough she could
fall through, opens
at our feet—my mind recalibrating
the day, the dangers
of our sunlit yard, all the gears
of disbelief and terror drilling down
through my chest, as I feel along the line
between horror and sense,
what to make of this—*an old well, perhaps!*,
and snatch her away.
Love's a hole we all fall through
to grief, a tenderness
ringed in terror. My girl, her beauty
blazing, waves the garden hose,
its spray a shifting
umbrella of rain,
perforating joy, each frame
broken and spliced to the next
for those of us who stay lit,
the deep brass note reverberating even now
below our keening birds, distant motors
gunning, the dappling light playing us
in minor key, before the trebled
silence of aspen leaves, the panning out, the curtain's fall.

The Dolls' House

When the diagnosis came in: stage four
metastatic cancer, I hauled the dolls' house
from my mother's basement, mouse dust
and damp pressed board. It was no small
feat, dragging our prized toy, a full
four feet tall, up my mother's stairs to scour
the wall paper with ammonia, to tear out
the tiny carpets seeded with droppings, to gut
the house she'd glued down with paint brushes
and toothpicks. I scrubbed till my sinuses
ached and, lightheaded, I nearly lost my footing.
Oh, hollow boarded room, aching
and stinging with astringent—
what am I but this womb, part miniature home,
part scoured box they'll lay my mother in?

Atrium

Mouse nest of fur and dry twigs, seashell-eardrum
Where the tide repeats and sea birds arc the sky, my heart

Wears the scrap of a robin's wing, smells of salt cliffs and campfire.
It carries under its tongue an old coin.

Thrumming its deadly circuit, my heart pumps slivers
Of a once-perfected glass egg, shards of my mother's wrist bones

Through veins thin as a bird's blue eye.
Papery, stone-smooth, dry as a wasp's nest,

It is vast as the eye of a needle,
Small as the lion-sun burning a hole in heaven,

Empty as a beaded purse, as an unhinged pocket.
My heart expects nothing, though, stupid child, it won't stop imagining

A full glass of water trembling in sunlight.
The waxy eucalyptus leaf unbraids to leaf rot.

Hope, the russet knife, enters the grillwork of ribs, my heart
A burst peach. Take it, my love, my reader, my nobody, into your hand,

And, like a split pomegranate, think it lovely.
I have been plying it with cyanide, and there, in the privacy of your palm,

It will bleed out, will fill all its chambers with dark matter.
Come reader, come beauty, come clean white sheet, we need none of it.

Invocation: A Fragment

The riptide's call, the willow's conflagration,
loss's swaddled robin. I could have loved you in my crenulated
dark, a flaw, globed and fingerprinted, a pearl beneath
my tongue. Instead, this plush dark. Come, emptiness,
the bell wired to its ring. Come, a field is burning in the sun.
Come, for loss is vagrant, is familiar as the body I live in.
Though I am staggered, I am not undone.

.. .. ..

The peonies have fallen into bloom again. What stupidity
          is desire: a thrush's call skating an empty sky,
the moon hanging like a strip of wallpaper, a lantern
          above a narrow bed, its wake,
endlessly exasperating circles beneath the water strider's six legs.

.. .. ..

A flock of birds enters me. They bring with them pewter vowel-tones,
cornhusk, salt-ache, cicadas rattling their ashy skins.

I have become bird-call, train-whistle, a two-note warble.

.. .. ..

Late winter my mother would watch for the first robin, *a sign of spring*,
she'd say, though it is the chickadee who trills the phantom of my childhood

back to me, its plaintive, insistent calling of its own name
on a high branch outside my bedroom window: *chickadee-dee-dee*, its call

my infinite fine-boned reflection in the medicine cabinet glass,
a stuttered desire of notes, a throat hollowed by hunger.

The Shower

Because she'd waited for me to arrive
to shower *just in case*, she said,
and because I'd driven ninety miles to hover
outside the bathroom door, gaping just enough
to allow the umbilicus of oxygen tubing in,
and because it reminded me of days
right after giving birth, my husband
standing outside the shower to hand me
our shrieking daughter, so she could draw from me
(who had nothing, but a new horizon
of blood scrim dividing self from self, to give,)
her consolation of milk as we wavered
and disappeared into the shower's scream, I went in,
feeling the backward pull of the oxygen tubing
running down the hallway to where my daughter
played by the generator, but pulled too, indelibly,
into the noise and steam of the bathroom,
where beneath our feet the floor was giving way,
the sub-floor worn through and dripping moisture radiant
with my mother's washed cells to the basement floor.
God of mourning, God of bright cells proliferating
down my mother's spine, what rain of abandoned love,
what wine of unfiltered air you christen us in,
you who give us to each other, curled and suckled,
small as the pressed nucleus inside its ring of fire.
Mother stood behind the curtain, her flagging
lungs unable to saturate her blood, her soapy head
slowly collapsing into bubbles on the shower wall.
I went in fully clothed, to link my arms beneath
her armpits, so she wouldn't crumple to the porcelain,
while she gasped and rinsed shampoo from her hair,
then I eased her to the toilet seat. Forgive me
my desire to shore up this house, brace the cracking
joists, shine the hardwood swollen with her step, as though,
somehow, I might recover her from body ash, smear
of hand cream, flush of milk on glass, her life simmering
inside its bright satellite, its luminous shell,
what the neighborhood kids called "the house
of a thousand windows." Now that is an empty glass
and she towed through some other conduit,
like the ferry to Nova Scotia,

a box of light crossing the sound, its boom announcing
an entrance into a granite sea, but it's sailing now out
beyond the Bay of Fundy, beyond Canada
through to the icy Atlantic, a medium black as glass,
and my mother, with her cool hands, rides it.

The Shutting

—after Caspar David Friedrich's "Seashore in Moonlight"

Like rising in the pre-conscious dark of a poem,
where the bubble of waking breaks
on sudden knowledge, terror
caught in the updraft,
Friedrich's terrible private seascape

becomes what you fear most
in the murky shallows of your mind
where tide-raked horrors dredged

appear. This was Friedrich's final seascape, the world
at the end of his life, the paint
so pitch it holds only the glimmer
of fish scales,
descending the tarry vaults.

Two centuries after his clouds hemorrhaged above him,
so that even the light of the moon's thin consciousness
was doused, what in this dark mirror do we see?

The piled dead, haloed in shade and floating
in dark tangles, billowing steel girders
folding like fans
falling like ash, families stranded
on roof shingles beneath the sky's clenched fist, or, simply

old age, my mother, thinned to bone
moving through the home
I grew up in, where

each year the cracks in the walls grow longer?
She's made up sheets on the sofa
where she sleeps before the violent weather
of the television screen. We can't move her
though we've tried,

her face rocky after a fall, the eye ringed
in a purple inner-tube. She's told a neighbor
she eats dinner from a can she's too tired to heat,

tells us she doesn't need a nurse at home, won't let her in.
I didn't know middle-age would be so hard
to navigate, that the sky would mirror
the sea's darkness and close
like a clamshell on us with our

rough square sails. Who knew
there would be no good answers?
The moral questions loom larger

each season, with greater consequence.
All day I stare at this painting,
Seashore in Moonlight, close my office door
and cry. After a stroke closed down one wing
of his mind and left his hand clawing

the phantom brush, Friedrich took up
the splintered wood a final time
to paint the belled darkness of our hearts.

His body halved, his mind already lightning-struck,
the shaking arthritic hand rose to paint
our final threshold. The mind at the end of its life
is a map under blackout,
one district after another gone blank.

See: his crippled, airless dark is ours—the frozen lake
spreading icy fingertips across the continents of his mind—
the dark of incapacity is ours, this new age, where,

by contraction, the gears of heaven and earth are closing—
no more *gold to airy thinness beat*, no more—
but only this opalescence, this pregnant shutting
where the horizon is a white streak
that squeaks through the hinge,

and the moon's light is a few white lines,
each growing increasingly shorter, Hope,
a diminishing triangle of light on the sea.

Apple of the Earth: A Fairytale

When the witch hazel snaps her paper lantern of seeds, each
flower is a bedraggled girl's head. Love's a stone well we—
        like the girl from my childhood,
        who cartwheeled from the bridge's balustrade—

might drown in. She somersaulted night's dark knowledge
before she broke her flowering stems.
        I used to wait until dark, sneak to the well, lift the lid,
        and draw just one sip to my lips, icy and tasting of night's shade.

Now the splintering lid's been plied back, and the well's one eye stares
all day and all night at infinite sky. I am exposed.
        The well is terrible. There my daughter and I are princesses.
        We walk its slippery rim, our hair

in plaits: mine thick and dark twines, hers golden snakes.
At dusk we are not alone. From the forest's shadow
        creep boys with sling shots and hard stones, the boys
        from my childhood who spat in my hair and grabbed

my breasts. My daughter
doesn't see them, though they are there. She doesn't see
        the man who watches us from the shadows of pine, the man
        with his myopic eye, his penchant for pornography.

She sees none of this and dreams of her prince. I am always cold.
During wartime my father carried a baked potato
        in his pocket. Hot from the coals, it radiated heat
        through wool all morning.

My daughter, too, radiates heat, my little *pomme de terre*. She
climbs onto my lap warm as love and smelling of butter.
        Some days we sing to the witch in the well,
        her hair in dark tangles, her heart ebony (while mine

is always breaking into flower). Tonight, from the gloaming
wood, the shadows are out again. Child of mine,
        rock me to sleep, while stars cartwheel the witch's cold broth,
        and, from the wood, the stranger's power grows.

Go

When D. said he'd had the impulse, thought it
        kindness to cover her face
in the goose down pillow, D. in all his clinical remove,
        wanting to stop her suffering,
and she, no longer able to swallow,
        her mouth stuck open,
a gurgling in the back of her throat, her voice
        taken and replaced
by a deep feathered silence, I felt
        the jump of pulse
in her neck, the kick as it thumped
        her hardening arteries,
the burst vessel bluing her temple,
        and knew then—after knowing all
those months she was dying—I wasn't ready,
        though I'd thought I was
rational as D. knowing the inevitable,
        which crests over all of us, was
cresting now over her, not ready and panicked
        in the undertow, a desperate need
to fight the great muscled ocean, my brother raising
        the pillow, the curls along his thick arms
graying, the great roiled undertow
        which pins us and blindly takes
all our unfathomable loves, our tender
        unmet needs and suffers them
to an abiding silence, my mother, her hands
        gripping the sheets where they'd
been folded, a grip so muted now, her whole
        bodily attention focused on continuance,
on beat and breathe, though I held her
        and cried, as they told me to,
and said, "You can go. It's okay, you can go."

Sanctuary: A Premonition

Birds unfurl like umbrellas, opening on morning,

Spires of cricket song trill the fog-cleared world,
Icicles cling to spring-laden fig trees,

And salt stings the world new. Your private road
Snakes a seaside mountain where, like barnacles, ice-lit rooms cling.

Each inner sanctum is beaded with chips of glass, panels, mosaics

Of thought. Finger this holy space, each lit closet, an asylum.

.. .. ..
.. .. ..

Gondolas snake the fissures, the canals strung with milky light.
Night water swirls each paddle stroke and, among the fish scales, nine moons float.

Sinkholes swallow vessels to the depth of pitch-marl,
But, if you weave with equilibrium, the temporal lobe

Is fire-sparked bands of cortex, riptide
And undertow, gulls riding a radiant periphery.

Muscled cranial nerves light this nether world, your private passages of sea.

.. .. ..
.. .. ..

Among the glowing sea anemones, among the spiked urchin and rising
Formless fears, I wove a tapestry

Radiant and discordant as true, but there at the patterned apex—
Through the subcontinent of dream figures—my own body rose, decorated

Cobalt to design the interior, russet
Marking my flesh with x's, where once an organ was lifted,

And everywhere the body I ghosted in my whole life
Was corseted in petunias, gardenias, gladiolas and bouquets of golden pears.

The umbrella mass

gelatinous, inscribed and curlicued
in fuchsia spun-glass ribbons tight beneath a glassy dome
is like candy, sweet to the eye,
its tentacles tickling

the lucent strata of ocean, the liquid layers more complex
and cut by light shafts into geometries
of consciousness, multidimensional,
through which gritty fish swim. Medusa, sensitive nerve-net

cap, skin thin enough for diffuse oxygenation,
deadly, lovely jelly streamers,
her bell contracted
in Fourth of July explosions,

is free, independent, bell-tongues undulating.
In the deep down a many-armed diver approaches:
flippered and masked, he, pregnant
with a complex electronic insect strapped to his belly,

appears to her an anglerfish, the filament dangling
from his forehead flashing camera-eyed,
photo sensors crawling
within his black box, stippling her image phosphorescent, lurid.

She knows the bioluminescence is a lure to bait her
and his decreasing concentric circles terrify.
He is a bottom-dweller and powerful:
she feels his net of electronic impulses

fall over her, her sensitive mushroom top, her rhubarb stalks,
the threads of her hair tangled now as, in a series
blooming contractions, she tries to rise.

Shadow Boxes

" . . . her poems are like his boxes, a place where secrets are kept"
—Charles Simic, on Emily Dickinson and Joseph Cornell

What will you do in this veiled chamber, this cloistered
interior, the rooms where secrets are kept?

See: interior with curio cabinet.
Open the glass doors: a clavicle, a coracle, a craft for prayer

of beech bark lashed with leather. Crenulated coral,
—run your fingers over each holy object—

the milky moon of stone, my eye socket.
The oracular icons of my subconscious, take them to your lips like words.

Fold out my mahogany secretary's desktop—
(you don't belong here)—the tiny internal bones of drawers,

ligaments of hinge and nail:
the leather-bound book where I keep my ovary,

the shoebox you refuse to open.
Come: interior with bird's nest and blue marble,

interior with drift wood, with revolving glass egg,
interior with sheet folded for the dead and robin's wind-swept wing.

Beneath the carpet—(peel it loose)—lift the trap door,
slip between the floor joists of the house,

down the ladder spining my crawl space,
to a dirt and graveled floor. Oh, the breached interior,

the smell of rain on stone! You are bent double,
here where seashells are worn to skeletal rings,

a wasps' nest is loosening great wings of bandages,
and the boxes, boxes each with its diorama of memory and dew.

Avert your eyes from the speculum on the dank floor,
the spectacular jaws of forceps.

What have they done with her? Why are we here?
A leathery fist fills my chest.

Everywhere the brains of unopened magnolia blossoms—
(Reader, can you bear it here?)—aching with their syringe-tips of loss.

Prayer

In meditation, in communion,
        the soul's desire offered
on a bedside tray: syringe-spirit of morphine,
        elixir of Abilify,
the bit of sponge to swab your mouth
        hollow now as a listening,
the wafer of a kiss to your forehead
        like a blessing, a prayer,
your six children in the disarray
        of grief arrayed
about your bed careful
        to loop the catheter
just so, so the distillation
        of fluids won't back up,
the plastic won't chafe, the ankles
        must hover above the bed.

Mother, I call this worship, I call
        this praise,
and when you said it, the one word,
        articulated with difficulty
the day sentences were lost,
        speech becoming
a thing of the past, the communion
        of voice disappearing
into a hazed darkness,
        and your youngest son,
the only Christian among us,
        prayed for you
in a startling foreign voice,
        you must, then,
have been white and pure as root
        knowing
you were leaving us
        against your will,
and for what, for silence, for
        a vast lethal
unknown, for the golden light of your
        childhood church,
or some recycling of souls?

I call this holy, the intimacy
        of terror, of letting another wipe
and clean you, your bluing forehead,
        your stiffening
body lifted by those who love you,
        the ritual worship
of caretaking, the bowed heads
        on your sheets,
the incense rising from your breathing masks,
        the sweet smell
of your room, of your last breaths
        as I climbed
in bed with you now beyond
        volition or voice,
holding your stiffness as I do my daughter
        within the comfort of sheets,
the rituals of purifying,
        of apology, your ardent love.

Night Aria on the Widow's Walk

The attic stairs' creak and sag, the dormer window's high cranny,
The night starring my widow's walk:

Cold heads of nails glisten in the mineral-dark, the basin
Pitted like a battered kettle.

You can walk out into this dark broth, this salty absence, but drink
The night-poison, and you will never be the same,

Always the dank pull to break the surface tension.
I know better:

I cling to the shingles, rain falling on the tin can roof,
Water buckets plashing tomato plants.

I have no power but that of observation.
His decision is his.

I cling to the high banister, and in the morning
Will tend to the potting shed,

The snag-toothed hoe, the ax, furrow the garden plot's dank soil.

But my cellar stairs lead to broken earth, spiders' nests,
The scullery cupboard smelling of mildew.

This house is old, old, old as my inheritance: this cathedraled-body,
Its vestibule lit with stained glass,

The stairs forever descending.
There I will search the toy cupboard I played in as a child,

The darkroom smelling of acid,
Burn cones of incense to spiral-ash,

The LPs spinning beneath diamond dust.
I will dig to see root-hairs,

I will crouch until I walk like an old woman, my hair feral as Medusa's.

Flame of pine needle, snare of chicken wire,
The fox's scarlet-scent.

My pendulum-heart clocks my parents' mantle.
Scatter wolfsbane, mint, braid lines of knotted garlic,

The TV antenna rattling like a divining rod, my mesoglea
A jellied amethyst, bloodstone and rose quartz.

Oh, the night terrors, the endlessly ringing phone,
Each window into his mind opens onto a new balcony, perverse

As a father's suicide,
But it is not *my* plaited head

He might sever; I
Will be terrible, my fire-tentacles burning a ring

Around my oral arms, my blood-lit brood pouches, my one egg sack.

A Toast

This is a toast to the crumpled sky
of bird shell in my daughter's bucket, its death-smear

of opened yolk, a toast to the snapped geranium's
tart spell, to this earth of mica chip and bone,

to crumbling brick, to love's broken face,
to the locust's glassy enunciated shell.

This is a toast to the suck of a hard kiss, to rivers
that run deep under stone,

to fetus-curling in my mother's hips,
to the thrum-pulse of her life's orbit,

to the white-ash hair I won't feel again,
to love's knotted and difficult end,

to loss, to calling it quits, to the silent diorama
of the heart, to sandboxes and sieves,

to the panorama of loneliness, to a well-lit
emptiness, to crying in public, to unspoken love,

to my tilled face, to what went wrong, to—
say it without artifice, this is a toast to divorce.

Morning after a Stormy Night

Tentacled, seething, the sea is roiled, smoking
salt-spray skyward where the morning breaks
on wreckage, a splintered raft, its guttered sail clinging
to the stone foot of great baked slabs of cliff-rock.
A single bell buoy teeters out to sea, its clarion call
eclipsed by the ocean's God-sound, its trumpeting of angels
at the end of the world, and, beneath the green glass boil,
the subconscious spirits of an underworld dredge
and moan. She'd spent the night fighting with her spouse,
the kind of fight made crueler by its uselessness
as if its only point were retribution for some forgotten
sin, the kind of fight in which the parameters of house
and yard become the cordons of some primal ring
where each is brutal and foolish beneath the kitchen lights,
and now in hindsight words spit like oil in the pan
of her mind, and she is awed by their complicity, the way each
drew the spearhead of meanness from the other
while their daughter slept. God of reason and passion,
of enlightenment and all that hunkers below, how do we
stay the burning coals when every heap of sand
seems rigged to explode, how do we turn the tide out to sea,
call in the seagulls to ride the swells on feathered haunches
back to shore, when the sky, shorn in bloodied sleeves of light,
flags in defeat of all it cannot reason with, and below
a single figure, contracted by degrees, spirals in on herself,
only a dog, attentive and long-tailed as love, at her feet?

Two.

Requiem

At the end of the hall, where my mother's room glows like an incubator,
        The night nurse, who, all last night watched TV

And drank soda after soda, her feet propped up, this morning
        Has drawn up a chair to study my mother's features, this woman

Who's seen hundreds shake in a dance of death, "terminal
        Agitation" it's called, then go root quiet,

A bulb beneath the bright lights of heaven,
        This woman whose son rose to the surface of the pool

In the cracked half-life of her dawn, his robe prostrate on the deck,
        She enters a cold and silvery knife each morning,

And each night she enters the rooms of the dying
        As if to see, with their kiln bright eyes, into both worlds:

Her son again, the glistening shape of him on the diving board
        In the candled dark, his shockingly muscled thighs strobing

The night pool . . . and I, in my urgency and my panic, ask
        What, in her expert's gaze, she sees—

The blue undertone of a minor chord drawn through the delicate bones
        Of my mother's face, a new stiffening of the living instrument's frame—

But she says simply, *She's drawing pretty bad now*, and I decide
        Breath, she means my mother's breath,

Her chin thrown back in oxygen need,
        Her skin sunk to the hourglass of bones, my mother clinging

To everything she knew, every blessing she'd been given,
        Her six children circling the bed in vigil, in prayer old

As death itself, as though all these years came down to this: an orchestra of syringes,
        Vials, masks and breathing treatment,

The lifting and lowering of our stiffening mother, we the shifting constellations
        Around a vanishing center.

Elegy with Fossilized Sharks' Teeth

My father's ashes drift
        the sunlit sea by Calvert Cliffs,
where as I child I saw him
        hardy and muscled, big
as the sea. I found nothing,
        though I searched all day,
hot and thirsty, stumbling
        on pebbles.
Little seedpod skulls swirled
        along the bluff
at lunchtime where we lay
        his old army blanket
to picnic. On his palm
        I remember
three perfect ebony triangles: fossilized
        sharks' teeth,
surprisingly small, not much larger
        than mine, but born up
through the black gums
        of that powerful animal.
Once, in the time of Pliny the Elder,
        these shards
were thought to have fallen
        from a fractured sky,
night shattered on the beaches.
        During the Renaissance,
they were thought to be
        the petrified tongues
of dragons. I wanted to put one
        in my mouth, but
my father taught me science:
        how water
infiltrates the body, eroding
        and ossifying
what once lived, replacing
        organic matter
with stone. Years later
        when the arteries,
which crowned
        my father's heart
like a wreath,

occluded to bony canals
and his voice rang in my ear,
as it rings even now
in my mind—
“if,” he is saying
“if, when everyone arrives,
I’m not here,
tell them
I’m so very sorry—,”
I took the Pennsylvania farm hills
way too fast, knowing
that great muscled mass
that had thumped under siege
through all my childhood,
and into my early middle-age,
now was water-logged,
lined with mineral deposits
hard as fossils,
and while my father,
sixty miles away in his bedroom,
in his last
animate moments, his
good heart open,
held his wife’s hand
and his sister’s,
stony tongues of dragons beat
my windshield
and the sky above me darkened
to a smoked glass vial.

Unraveling Her Web

Is it for love, this careful unspooling, slipping each slipknot
through its tiny noose, or is it simply the desire for stasis—
a hummingbird drumming its mad paper wings?
But no matter what she does, thirty approaches, the lovely
white skin of her sleeping son beside her, his arms lengthening
nightly into his future. It's hardest, she knows,
to know one's own motivation, and Odysseus
has been gone so long she no longer expects his long
lean prow to divide the ocean. They call her
industrious and faithful, exquisite in her mourning, the colors'
shimmering pathos veining the wing of tapestry
she distills by firelight back to skein. Of course, it is to forestall
the men snuffling like boar around her windowsill
but mostly to be for as long as she can this woman married
to the son she can no longer take to her breast, because if she lets it happen,
lets the sun pleat each day to the fine fabric of her face, then
someday she will have to leave him, not Odysseus
who has already left, but this boy she spooned from her body,
this boy who lengthens each day, his arms hanging from sleep
reaching to take the world by the mane, this boy who in her arms
is heavy as the dusk-blue sky, and to leave him
is a pain too exquisite to suture with any thread.
She'd cleave the surgeon's blade through her belly
to birth him again, the miracle of his life and hers steaming
like a butcher's shop, if only it meant this,
this moment in the glow of night, the burlap shadows
making a pocket for them finite as her womb
before the perforating, her skin a bolt of cloth
beneath shears, but *enough*, she thinks
unpicking each eyelet and focusing instead on each miniature embrace
of thread looping thread, *keep those thoughts at bay*,
though even now light breaches the sky's sack of waters,
and out beyond the camp border, wolves begin
their serenade, the wool holding beneath the crochet hook,
unfastening and holding again and, beside her, beneath
the membrane of eyelids, Telemachus begins his descent into day.

Adoration

"A vessel always retains the smell of the first liquid that it contained."
—Wayne Franits, on 17th century childrearing

Heavy on her knees she's swept the hearth with hog bristles,
the hardwood with broom corn, the Delft tiles with flax and horsehair.
The kettles she's burnished, the vats for mutton and pork,
but it is the water vessel she loves best, its lovely dented copper
fitted to her flat palm and the way water pours pure as the spill
of fine wheat flour. It contains only the coppery scent of spring water
risen from agate, slipping in her memory over her daughter's newborn form:
that first animal cry untying the ribbon in her breast, milk running
through her shirt, her own heart thrumming over, the bile flushed
from all her pores until, two inches from her scalp,
her hair under the scarf was soaked with it. Oh, to flush the bile
from the whole world's body, and to fill it instead with the sanguine
pats of butter she prepares for her daughter's rye bread!
This love drives her to scour and draft and parch.
She is always on her knees before this girl; she'd throw her hair
in the dirt in adoration. If only the world would do likewise, but crimson
casts the windowpanes, catches in her husband's shirts outside on the line,
moves in the bed linens. It sharpens the knitting needles at her breasts,
and she knows too well to believe her daughter safe
beyond the microcosm she daily scours, the swept cave of her heart
where only candlelight ticks her daughter's fine skin.

A Woman Weighing Gold

—After Pieter de Hooch

She is up early, weighing the household gold,
the wall's worn damask gilt in the rising sun.
Under the minute attention of this privileged hour
and the moon of the clockmaker's glass, she sees
the ducats cunningly clipped. This marketplace
sleight of hand, the traveling charlatans
will threadbare her children's calicos. The girls'
gingham dresses must become half-sleeved blouses,
their lengthening wrists dangling. On the western side
of the house, they drift in the warmth of their bodies,
limb-tangled. She loves to lie with them, the smell
of the air from their lungs deeper than torn pine limbs,
but their slumber eludes her. Oh, to enter that privileged
space! Anxiety slices the rind of her sleep, enters her seeded
interior, and she wakes wet in the bedclothes, rises
to a household eroding to her husband's soiled silks. Each crease
holds its secret in the washtub she rakes them through.
Even the cat's coat in tatters, he strokes her mornings
like no one else, warmer than the fires banked in the stove
and vibrating his living frame. All exits are complicated; shadows
bar the vestibule. Once she loved that entryway's leaded-glass,
but today how its perspective jeers at her! : the interior doors,
the exterior doors, a jerrybuilt gate and the alleyway
to the marketplace where all life—caged, stunted or strung up—is for sale,
the booths of skinned rabbits, pheasant carcasses ready for plucking
in her kitchen and, oh, the hens soon to be throttled,
their opalescent eggs waiting like ducats in each man's oiled purse.

Woman and Child Blowing Bubbles

The pig's bladder she takes to her lips and fills like a lung,
slips in shiny pebbles, a plaything
for her daughter to rattle over tiles. They say she spoils her,
and her daughter's sleeves drip wet lace,
as they dip dinner utensils through dishwater to spray bubbles
through the kitchen gloom. The dog her daughter manhandles
with a love rough as any boy, though when she holds this child,
they both go limp with need. How she loves to be coddled,
to be told she is perfect, precious, all the things you are not to tell
your children for fear they will think they are owed
all pleasures, the split carcasses strewn across her butcher's block,
the mincemeat pies broken open on her table, the sweets stacked
and canned in the cupboard. But she knows no girl
turned to whoring for the love of meat, only the girls at the tavern
too starved to know their own need, teeth broken on brutality.
So she coddles her daughter, who begs her
each morning to play, play rather than fill the wash tub,
and her girl is strong-willed, that is true, and can throw a storm
of a fit which rattles the neighbors, but she is sharper
than the tomato knife, keener than the serrated grapefruit spoons
they use some nights when they sit out back, scooping the sweet-tart
slices to their mouths. Clinging to her mother's broadcloth, her girl knows
nothing of the marriage bed, but perhaps, her mother thinks,
with a mind like that and the will besides, she'll find a way
to fill the ballooning emptiness, rattling like knuckle bones at every woman's ribs.

The Lace-Maker's Bloom

Lace muffles the warming trays, so when her children
come to her, faces cross, hair ratted by schoolyard
bullying, she can fill them with bacon drippings, potatoes
flavored with lard, chunks of warm cheese.
The door knocker, too, she's muffled in lace, an announcement—
to anyone who comes to the splintering door—of the birth,
this child milk-heavy in her dress or rocking, as she is now,
by her foot. Oh, the industrious hour of near solitude, her foot working
the treadle of the cradle, her mind cooling blank but for the blue square
of the lace maker's pillow, the hundred bobbins,
the linen thread's torque and tighten! How she loves the cell
of quietude, this caesura in which no infant shrieks, no child pulls
hard on the apron of her mind, and the whole universe is paused for
there is no husband here in this moment to rave the seams of her chest
open, only this careful darning-up, loop, twist, cross, over someone else's
pattern, and it's lovely, it's lovely, it's lovely! This cauliflower lace collar
can turn her daughter's coarse dress fine. And how it sells
on the market; they all want it, what she can do up in an hour's
peace, the threads liquid in her fingers, drips of chartreuse, inky
blood-red and the many, many humors of blue. Let the churchmen
call it trivial, vanity, the lace which decorates frock fronts and dresser tops,
the oh-so-easily-torn veil of pillowcase. She calls it beauty, and isn't
that what beauty is, that which conceals and reveals in patterns spun
like bloom: a net the finer spun, the more easily rent. It's nun's work, too,
she'd like to tell them, and she knows it, the nun's meditation,
the body lax but for the fingers' focus, the fine singing
of her fingers through a web, *chrysanthemum, chrysanthemum*.

In the Garage

Despite the oxygen tank that now went everywhere
        with her, he was afraid she'd code in the garage,
the exertion of having struggled from wheelchair
        to car too much, and he,
as a doctor, would have to perform CPR
        in front of his children, which would mean breaking all her ribs—
and what would they feel,
        seeing him straining over their grandmother
on the stained garage floor, the sickening
        crunch and then the rise,
suddenly menacing, sweat lining
        his upper lip—and so,
as her anxiety rose to thinning altitudes, Nick ran
        and turned on a second oxygen generator,
the backup in the dining room, and ran back again
        with the tubing draped through the kitchen
out through to the garage to where my mother was gasping
        in the car and fitted
a second canella into her nose, *not exactly standard*
        procedure, he later said, and said, *Breathe, close*
your lips and breathe, as I'd heard him
        instruct her so many times before, *Your saturation*
is rising, he'd say, reading numbers from
        the monitor he'd clipped to her finger,
and he saved her, my brother, one
        shimmering coin of oxygen hitting her bloodstream
at a time, *seventy-seven*, the bubbles
        beginning to rise to her surface, the blue cast
easing to grey, and my mother
        returned, terrified, to the garage and the sounds
of children calling
        to meet her son's gaze, her beautiful son who,
she'd told me two weeks before,
        tucks me in each night, and how many mothers
can say that of their sons?,
        the bright disks of their love sinking into her,
his wife's, the children's
        silver high-pitched laughs falling on her
like the sunlight on the well now

that she is dead and my daughter stands,
her hands full of bright coins she is pitching
into the shopping mall's wishing well: *this one*, she's saying, holding
her dime aloft, *this one is important*,
the glassy tile beneath her suddenly slick
so that I want to snatch her away,
I wish, she's saying triumphantly,
a shimmering net of reflected lights
riding the pool's glossy surface, *when we die*
we see Grandma Marilyn again, and beneath us
tons of cement and mortar and stone
hold the huge mall in place, beneath that
bedrock and bone, and compressed into the earth's
core, streams and flint, mica and sand silt
slipping, my hand now gripping my daughter's bare
shoulder, as she's at the very edge, the world
tilted and too bright so that we
and all the crowd
with its many individual shopping bags
are on a cliff's edge, salt spray sharpening our senses and below
the sea crashes as it did at Seawall in Bar Harbor
when I was a girl, my hand in my parent's, the thrilling thunder
of waves crashing
the sheer stone alcove so that my voice
could not be heard, relentless, thunderous, pounding
all the delicate sea creatures
to grit, sodium and tentacle.

The Legible Body: or Melancholia

It is 1842 and Napoleon has returned to Paris
as body-ash grey as the iron Seine,
Fuseli and Lavater have worked all winter painting
the soul's character to flesh, each high forehead
a cathedral vaulted for the mind,
and in Italy Francesco Hayez paints this girl,
not so much a portrait as a study, the oval
of her face flattened and white as a cameo.
He paints her disheveled as the rumpled flowers
he places before her as if she, too, were perfumed
to lush disintegration, her bodice a waxy sheet
draped to falling, the lilies enveloped
in their private fluted mouths. He extends no grace
to her, but lets the light from one window
cut down the side of her face, her dress
pooling as if he can't help himself, can't stop
unlocking in his mind the pearly sheen
of each elasticized button, though she is sullen
and slouched as any preteen, awkward
in her new layers, and, in the muddied pools of her eyes,
he paints the whole of her psyche in concentric rings,
at once over-taxed as her mother and extravagantly
swollen, a child in the mane of her disillusionment.
Even the cross he gilds mid-fall, but she doesn't catch it,
doesn't rearrange herself like a girl at the pool
tugging up her suit, no, her hands
are stiff in her dress, listless to deformity.
Her face is like one who will take a beating
without flinching, and isn't that what this is,
as she stands for him who cowers behind the screen
of his canvas, he who props her up
before the blank brick and tugs the dress
from alignment, convincing himself he's caught her
in her undressed mind, this girl for whom
martyrdom means holding very still
that he can make of her madness and sex?
In another century, a poet thinks himself
the wind God and she the harp he'll run the string
of his breath through like bell-song, and like Chloris

she lies for him, a burnished shell, her cones
filling with his notes, though before long
his flora clots in her throat, blood-flakes fern
from her lips, and her own sound is stopped, guttural
in her long white throat. What a familiar myth
they enacted before the stone and ivy walls of Cambridge,
1956, his arm yoking her as it would for seven years,
her girlish smile, light trolling the shadows. Here solidity
is defined by her vanishing, the aural white;
he grows larger as she less palpable. Must there always be
a vanishing twin in this unnatural partnership,
or else the two-headed monster they became when she spoke,
anger ticking in her throat? Hayez called his portrait *Melancholia*
as though he knew her, knew what darkened her pupils
to crushed pencil points was desire for annihilation, but it was he
who wanted to see her ripe for the taking, as if there were nothing
more to do with her but lift the seashell-blue
of her dress and punish her as she asks to be punished.

Prayer 2

When I addressed that secret kernel in my heart,
that knot like an eye in the needle of me,

the primitive place I hardly name but speak to,
and prayed aloud, as I'd never done before,

your hands struggled together in a child's
reflex of prayer, and I found myself saying, *God,*

this is too much, because I needed the frantic terror
to stop the way I'd needed to stop Chloe's colicky cry

with my nipple, a need so strong I couldn't
think or eat or sleep, but needed with a blind

impotence to hold back what might be pain or terror
in the spirals of her heart, the vast black cloak of the universe

spinning around us, menacing and arbitrary
as the rickety mechanisms of a carnival ride

which probably won't crash while the one you love—
like lightning across the sea of your consciousness—rides it

screaming in the throes of delight, but relies only
on spinning wheels, a generator, worn cogs, the unthreading screws

of starlight, so when the poultice of my hands
wouldn't heal you, when all our routines of comfort,

our spreadsheets of medications carefully checked off,
couldn't bring you back to us or stop the agitation, your hands

picking at air as if stitching one moment to the next
against a palpable unraveling, the terror unbearable,

and because, though you begged us to, we couldn't
save you, I prayed, then, for your death,

while deep in your cerebellum
you sent out one order after another, *breathe, breathe,*

breathe, dragging now to every twenty seconds, *don't let go*,
your lungs drawing more ether than air, and, yes,

terrible as the evening sky purpling like a blood clot
above us, I asked the awful dark to take you, and, drafting

your room one light pixel at a time through to dark, it did.

Cartography

—after a Portrait of Madame Recamier, by Jacques-Louis David, 1800

Looking at us through the prism of her own interiority,
the almond-sliver of her face alert, intelligent,
she has the rich interior,
what Freud tried to elicit from his patients

years later, cluttering his studio like an archeological dig
of the subconscious, as though each silver inlaid lock-box,
each medallion, each figurine, sword,
might correspond to an inner trope, buried deep

in the womb of the mind. The mind, he knew, could be mapped,
like the world with its intoxicating scents, ships sailing
always for the east, one hand fingering
the fringe of occidental drape where a patient reclines,

her subconscious rising like beaded-oil
to the surface. But here in the painting, this woman
needs none of it, and although the painter has elongated her
into an elegance the body rarely possesses, she glances

at us only briefly, before turning back to the blank wall.
What a simple set he's devised!
The only props: a daybed to echo the curvature of spine,
two cushions, one a faded silk-blue, the other mustard seed,

and an oil lamp to suggest the far east, but otherwise the room is bare;
this is no Harem, this is not the artist's private thrill.
No, here we have a woman whose mind is untouchable
pure and clear agate, the top layers luminous,

the under-strata seen to none but her.
When the aura of theater lights fills her mind
and she feels the heat-flutter of bodies move across her stage,
she needs nothing and no one from this world

where men ask women to sit for them in fantasy,
        and she makes of that interiority this vibrancy—figures slipping
                down hallways to smaller and smaller rooms,
        and beyond the corridors opening onto miniature bricked pathways,

beyond the swinging bridges, beyond porticoes and creaking porch steps,
        her *self* is a filament of sunlight
                on a splintered oak table
        where a vase of tulips glistens by a curtain's raveled hem.

The Portrait Miniature

Focused down to a wafer,
a disk of enamel or ivory, thinned
by distraction but rich in miniature, the tiny,
deft red lines, full-bodied strokes
diminishing to point: it's no wonder
women wore them, tiny wombs,
pinned to the collar or slung at the throat.
They knew what it is
to be contracted to a bezel
and to hold in the luminous O of one's self,
the figure limned in amniotic light.
But here the girl—like sunlight emulsified,
apple-cheeked, the brittle laid paper pressed
like a gem-cutter's stone, the strata limned
with genetic accretion—is dust-sealed
beneath convex glass, embryonic, funereal,
a pinned butterfly caught in-loop between presence
and absence within a filigreed casket
pressed to cut-notch pulse
of her mother's throat. Here the dead
is rendered miniature to fit the jewelry box
of the heart. And look, on the back, a lock
of her hair, silky ash brown, knotted in gold thread
and saved—how long? a century!—reminds me
of the envelope of my own daughter's hair, her musky
honey blond, stored for her in my top desk drawer.
The pendant is a doll's house, domestic, yes,
but heavy as a pocket watch in the palm and
set on black so that beyond its gold rim
volutes of black cloth unveil the universe's
winding sheet, the mourning which sets each love
like a gem. I see the fine lace of pinholes thrown
across my daughter's skin as through a jeweler's glass,
and by the nightlight's glow, my body tries to make of itself
a rare atmosphere around her fine carnality,
a crystalline rim, the smell of sweat and soil unfolding
her center, like terrra deep in the womb
of the universe, the concentric rings of banded muscle
opening outward as they do in Renaissance prints of the cosmos,

the outermost ring flanked by God's whole chorus.
If only we believed in the twenty-first century
of fitting in a palm, the world a lovely wooden toy
with hidden clockwork gears and spinning horses.
If only I could lock like a Fabergé egg around this golden hen
carrying, in the carrying case of her own pelvis,
her tiny crown of rubies; instead I have become a woman
in her own daguerreotype, stiff and formal. The miniaturist's
finely worked metal, rose gold over copper is, too, the skull,
and if you let it, if you let the plates of the skull grind
too close, the threaded pin door lets no one in.

The Body: or Breach

Temporal, worldly,
but prone to weaknesses
of mind and character (lecherous,
they say, and gluttonous),
opposed to the spirit world
and starry constellations
of thought, riding always
the horizon of the sea,
that surface tension a hand
can rupture between air
and substance, though my daughter's
body is egg heavy,
a tremulous shell
spiraling inward, her home
suited and sleek, a styrofoam bubble
strapped to her back
as she dances on one leg
on the pool stairs: *buoyant*,
she's saying, bouncing, her new word,
I'm buoyant, and she is,
all new growth, her cells dividing,
bones lengthening, the fibers
of muscles tearing and rebinding,
the bubbles of self rising up
out of the deep-chambered tidal pull, climbing
a ladder of chromosomes, her body
spiritual and animal, carnal,
ethereal.
And all the while
inside of me, my mother's body,
re-membered through grief,
is a martyr, beyond reason, tortured,
shaking on the bedside commode,
calling me what I'd called her as a child,
Mommy, she's saying
clinging to me, *I'm so sick*, *so sick*,
and me, by some reflex
mumbling, *Mommy*, *I'm sorry*, *so sorry*,
until I don't know

who's who, or what mistake
        we are making: she thinking I'm her mother
or me participating in some regression
        or inversion,
that she's become me mothered
        by her, a great need
spreading out across the universe
        of our sky, bringing us
to our knees, humbling us
        beyond selfhood, so that it no longer matters
who is who, except that one of us
        is dying perpetually inside of me,
as I will someday and my daughter, the word, *Mommy*,
        a mantra, a prayer, a call for help
impotent as any call for help,
        her own mother dead and unable to save
her, as I, in this moment, save my own daughter, lifting
        her terror-filled face she accidentally spills
into the pool, the way in fantasy I believe,
        briefly, my mother's mother might
lift her as she dips through the wet
        scrim of this world and receive her
on the other side, she who abandoned
        my mother, she who, in life,
left her as everyone left her, and I can't do it,
        I can't be on the other side
to receive my mother, who's breaking
        even now through the membrane
inside me, so who will?

The Beekeeper's Daughter

She called them cat's eyes, the jelly jars
gleaming in the amber dark of the cellar,
slit with their pupil honeycombs, and each *was*
a kind of dormant consciousness eyeing her
in the dark, a papery brain catacombed
and crawling within its own waxy cells,
a subconscious like the cellar itself, brooding
beneath the floorboards. She must have felt
a kinship among the canning, the smell
of soil weathering in the press of splintered wood.
It was there, beneath the floorboards of her mother's womb,
she curled back into the sealed hive of herself
choosing that crawlspace as her hibernaculum.
Her four dragon wings sealed close about her abdomen,
she burrowed into the ash-grey of her wintering,
her heart a grain of sand slowing within the shell
of her exoskeleton, as if she might, like her father's
queen bee, emerge, months later, *resplendent*
among the buffalo currant's golden flagons. But
it was the bald inquisition light of the hospital
she returned to, the small sucking mouths tugging away
her old self, rancid as placenta, and as the crinoline walls
of the hospital parking garage gave way to the unbearably rare air,
Sylvia held in her mind the young Bombus queen
fatted and fresh from hibernation, the one, she'd read
in her father's journal, he'd cupped in the tenderness of his palm
a full mile that she might, in his garden—
grasping with her third set of legs, insert the tip of her abdomen
—her sting—into each egg-cell. Hermaphroditic, nearly
self-sufficient, the queen, Sylvia knew, was a sex all herself:
she need mate only once, and from her a whole colony stirs,
one egg-cell at a time, waxy, itching from her mandibles.
The drones, those dull bores, they wait by the hive entrance
for a virgin to emerge still drunk from the dark hive of birth
and rocket to her beginning the cycle: the bodies
of common bees littering the ground,
her former self—the founding queen, wings torn now
by the long foraging flights—gone to die,
and the young queen, the only genetically prepared

for the holocaust of winter, cocoons in radical isolation
preparing for her second birth and the hive
she will make in the spring of her life, the microcosm
of papery cells she alone can build with her six legs,
her twitchy abdomen, her sting impregnating each egg-cell.
I like to think of Sylvia at her desk stippling with care thought
to under-thought, eliciting from the mind something more than itself,
each poem a many-segmented architecture where
the subconscious and biological stir,
her vast focus building a nest of cells, so that
the manuscript she left when she died
became an engine throttling, a great papery mind
sibilating even now within its corrugated husk.

The Telephone Call

While you were working your way up
        to tell me what had happened, I,
in a panic to return to my mother
        slipping through the vestibule
of her thoughts, down the chambers
        of her cerebellum, implored you
to *just say it, say* what the college website
        wasn't, say what the press release
hadn't, though it had hinted, because my mother
        had entered the anteroom
of her dying,—a shooting
        a block from where my daughter
lies in the still bubble of her room,
        a student, dangerous, barred
from campus, and now this—*say it*
        before the siphoning world
we cling to bursts into flame *say*
        that my student has taken
to another's throat a knife, slashed
        her flesh
we don't know how many times, that
        he strangled her
while her pulse still beat like a bird
        in her throat, like my mother's
in her neck, though she's sunk now
        to where I can't reach her,
but fill her cheek with a morphine
        her gums can absorb,
so that below the constriction of muscle,
        her toes stuck pointed, her mouth
caught in a yawn, she won't feel the pain
        creeping the ladder of consciousness,
but can sink or rise now without pain
        to wherever it is
she's going and can take this girl dying
        the same day, this girl
I passed in hallways of the living, dead
        now by my gentle
student, and draw her as if by the lily stalk

of hand, from where
she's been stuck like a flag
above the spreading
shadow of body, the two of them
low flying planes
through my consciousness tonight,
the world suffocating us,
my mother's lovely hands, familiar
as my own, folded
across her lap while the undertakers
I can't look at, take her,
their taillights twin aircraft
riding an absolute dark.

Horse and Rider

—After George Stubbs' painting, "Horse and Lion"

She has been caught mid-stride
and, in a moment, she will be down on her knees, death
spooling red silk from her side.
Now her flanks flare like a ship's hull,
and, barreling through air thick as water,
blood thrumming her chest cavity, she torques—mid-air—
toward death riding her, hip to haunch, mane
to her velvet cheek, dragging his nails
through her withers. The day sets
across the crags of her wilderness, rivers veining
the length of her living continent,
and the sun paints her
creamy caramel-gold, her hair platinum,
as she, in a final agitation, rears, struggling to rise
from the in-home hospital bed,
but the whole of this black drama
is siphoned as if up the wicked-lean muscle of the lion's tail,
and there is nothing for her to do
but let death ravish her, its staccato
vise hold, a labor the body must move through.
What black hole, what cyclone updraft draws us all
to our deaths? What force rides us sidesaddle,
my mother lifting the whole of her skeleton
against the black-gloved fist, the whip bearing down?
What lusty God sits brooding behind his sublime screen
of wind whipped trees, stony outcroppings,
the blue and bubble white of his sky?

Effacement

If you labor within the foghorn of hospital lights,
    Distant voices from the nurses' station tinkling like Christmas bulbs
While you are wracked in the vise-grip of the sea,

Until the radial, final call breaks through their reverie
    And the delivery room emergency sirens rise in a locust swarm,
The four walls flashing and throbbing like the inside of a lighthouse:

Yourself awash within the over-taut
    Rib-and-timber hull of the body rocked to its broken side—
And if, from beneath the C carved across your underbelly,

The baby is ladled, and if she is unplugged, cleaned
    Of the tarry mucus of the underworld; If that child
Becomes your personal siren

Breaking her light across your driveway nightly;
    If she is lavender and widow's shriek,
The grind of interlocking gears, forceps piercing tissue paper;

If she is beautiful as pinecones distilled to tree skeletons
    And her needles imprint the floor of your mind—
If she is your cradle, your shell-case, and she rocks you to sleep

Beneath the scarring night sky, if she is an amber drop
    Clinging to your severed limb
Burning a constant flame, she is your pilot light,

Your lodestar, and you, thin as a compass needle, hover
    Always toward morning, toward east
Where she rises, slips off her skin and dances in her dragon-body full of luck.

Interior with Calder Mobile

—After Elizabeth Bishop

She painted interiors mostly, domestic spaces,
slightly old-fashioned, simple and practical,
places you could make-do comfortably
a month or two, an uncle's cabin with its potbelly stove,
a kettle, a spindle chair, flowers like pussy willows branching
from a water glass and, strangely,—in the air
a mobile—a Calder turning
like thought, like the movement of the mind
as floating color, a crescent blue,
two spheres on parallel planes,
a red cut-out like an eye, as if the imagination
might inscribe beauty over this city of sewage drains,
cable-car houses, municipal buildings and suicides unleashing
their bright death-balloons, as if the imagination
might, like cumulus cherry-blossom clouds, amass,
in the lowering spring sky,
then rain silky fingerprints across our backs, thought
hovering apart from the cast iron clangor of the mind.
Then, of course, there might be a soul, and when
the body loses its flock of birds to dismemberment, then,
perhaps, a single feathery thing remains, preening in the rain.

Notes

"The Shutting": the phrase "gold to airy thinness beat" is borrowed from John Donne's "Valediction, Forbidding Mourning."

"The umbrella mass": pays homage to Marianne Moore. My poem is inspired by a photograph of a medusa jellyfish approached and photographed by a deep-sea diver.

"A Toast": is indebted to Dana Gioia's "The Litany," as well as Rebecca Dunham's "This is a Letter."

"The Legible Body: or Melancholia": references Francesco Hayez's painting "Melancholia," as well as a photograph of Ted Hughes and Sylvia Plath.

"The Beekeeper's Daughter": quotes lines from Sylvia Plath's father's diary. Otto Plath was a zoologist.

Acknowledgments

I would like to thank the editors of the following journals where these poems first appeared or are forthcoming, sometimes in slightly different versions.

Blackbird: "A Woman Weighing Gold," "Woman and Child Blowing Bubbles," "Adoration"

Boulevard: "The Shutting," "The Shower"

Literary Imagination: "Horse and Rider"

Meridian: "Shelley on His Funeral Pyre," "Effacement"

New Letters: "A Toast"

Nimrod International Journal: "The Lace-Maker's Bloom"

North American Review: "The Beekeeper's Daughter," "Prayer 2"

Prairie Schooner: "Cartography," "The Body: or Breach"

Ploughshares: "Interior with Calder Mobile"

Shenandoah: *The Washington and Lee University Review*: "The Legible Body: or Melancholia"

Southwest Review: "Morning after a Stormy Night," "Shadowboxes"

storySouth: "The Dolls' House," "Go"

The Missouri Review: "Atrium," "Invocation: A Fragment," "Sanctuary: A Premonition," "And then"

The Southern Review: "The Portrait Miniature," "Unraveling Her Web"

Western Humanities Review: "Night Aria on the Widow's Walk"

I feel deep gratitude to those who have helped make this book a reality: Bill Olsen and Kim Kolbe who believed in this book, chose it miraculously, and ushered it into the world. I am grateful to Sarah Elizabeth Kidd for her careful and helpful editing. My wonderful poetry group has given me companionship, thoughtful generous feedback, and has nourished my writing life for many years: Emily Tuszynska, Eric Pankey, Jennifer Atkinson, Emily Lu and Melanie McCabe. Stephen Stern supported and believed in me, energetically cheering me on whenever I was discouraged. Most importantly, my daughter, Chloe, herself a budding writer, has sustained me with her love and joy every day as I wrote this book.

photo by Picture People

Nadine Sabra Meyer's first book of poems, *The Anatomy Theater*, won the National Poetry Series and was published by HarperCollins. Her poems have won the New Letters Prize for Poetry, the *Meridian* Editor's Prize, and a Pushcart Prize. Nadine holds a B.A. from Johns Hopkins University, an M.F.A. from George Mason University and a Ph.D. from the University of Missouri, Columbia. Poems from *Chrysanthemum, Chrysanthemum* have appeared in *The Southern Review, Southwest Review, Shenandoah, Literary Imagination, Boulevard, Nimrod, North American Review, storySouth, The Missouri Review, Prairie Schooner, Blackbird, Western Humanities Review* and *Ploughshares.* Nadine is an Associate Professor of English and Creative Writing at Gettysburg College.

The Green Rose Prize

2016: Nadine Sabra Meyer
Chrysanthemum, Chrysanthemum

2015: Bruce Cohen
Imminent Disappearances, Impossible Numbers & Panoramic X-Rays

2014: Kathleen Halme
My Multiverse

2013: Ralph Angel
Your Moon

2012: Jaswinder Bolina
Phantom Camera

2011: Corey Marks
The Radio Tree

2010: Seth Abramson
Northerners

2009: Malinda Markham
Having Cut the Sparrow's Heart

2008: Patty Seyburn
Hilarity

2007: Jon Pineda
The Translator's Diary

2006: Noah Eli Gordon
A Fiddle Pulled from the Throat of a Sparrow

2005: Joan Houlihan
The Mending Worm

2004: Hugh Seidman
Somebody Stand Up and Sing

2003: Christine Hume
Alaskaphrenia
Gretchen Mattox
Buddha Box

2002: Christopher Bursk
Ovid at Fifteen

2001: Ruth Ellen Kocher
When the Moon Knows You're Wandering

2000: Martha Rhodes
Perfect Disappearance